# Delicious Desserts

## Bobbie Kalman

### Crabtree Publishing Company

www.crabtreebooks.com

## Created by Bobbie Kalman

For my beautiful new grandson Liam, born against all odds
It was love at first sight!

**Author and Editor-in-Chief**
Bobbie Kalman

**Editors**
Kristina Lundblad
Kathryn Smithyman
Molly Aloian

**Art director**
Robert MacGregor

**Computer design**
Samantha Crabtree

**Production coordinator**
Heather Fitzpatrick

**Production assistant**
Katherine Kantor

**Food preparation and recipe-testing**
Kristina Lundblad
Valerie Martin

**Illustrations**
Barbara Bedell

**Special thanks to**
Erika Olarte, Jennifer Olarte, Valeria Olarte, Clara Godoy, Federico Olarte, Jayson Foster, Adrienne Foster, Aimee Lefebvre, Alissa Lefebvre, Sophie Izikson, Martin Izikson, Sara Paton, Joan King, Jonathan King, Chantelle Styres, Andrew Key, Alexis Gaddishaw, and Kristina Lundblad, my excellent assistant chef!

**Consultant**
Valerie Martin, Registered Nutrition Consultant, International Organization of Nutrition Consultants

**Photographs**
All photographs by Bobbie Kalman except the following:
Marc Crabtree: cover (bottom right), back cover (top), pages; 4 (top), 5 (bottom), 6 (top), 9, 10 (bottom), 16 (top), 17 (bottom), 18-19, 20 (bottom), 23, 29 (top left), 31 (top right)
Other images by Comstock and PhotoDisc

**Digital prepress**
Embassy Graphics

**Printer**
Worzalla Publishing

## Crabtree Publishing Company

www.crabtreebooks.com     1-800-387-7650

| | | |
|---|---|---|
| PMB 16A | 612 Welland Avenue | 73 Lime Walk |
| 350 Fifth Avenue | St. Catharines | Headington |
| Suite 3308 | Ontario | Oxford |
| New York, NY | Canada | OX3 7AD |
| 10118 | L2M 5V6 | United Kingdom |

Cataloging-in-Publication Data
Kalman, Bobbie.
  Delicious desserts / Bobbie Kalman.
    p. cm. --  (Kid power)
Includes index.
Summary: Presents recipes for sweet treats that are high in taste and nutrients, low in fat and sugar, and contain no sweeteners or artificial ingredients.
  ISBN 0-7787-1254-0 (RLB) -- ISBN 0-7787-1276-1 (pbk.)
  1. Desserts--Juvenile literature. [1. Desserts. 2. Cookery.]
I. Title. II. Series.
TX773.K27 2003
641.8'6--dc22
                                                    2003016195
                                                    LC

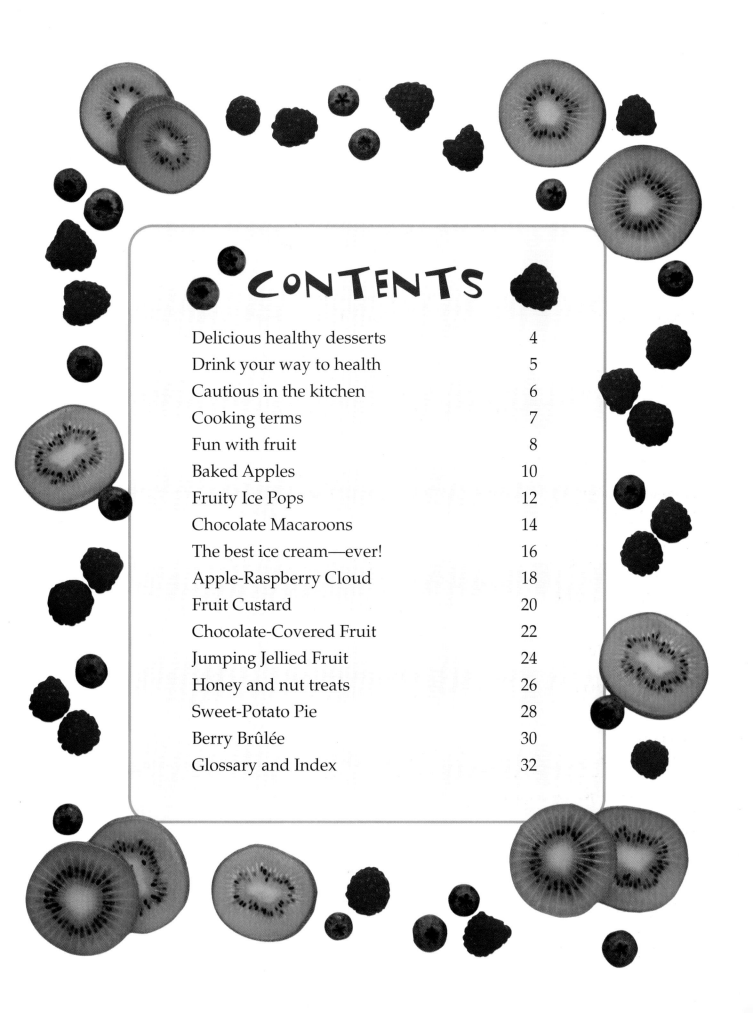

# CONTENTS

# DELICIOUS HEALTHY DESSERTS

Desserts are extra food treats we give ourselves. They taste good because of the fat and sugar they contain. Both of these ingredients can be challenging to our health. So, should we not eat desserts? We can probably live without them, but who wants to? This cookbook challenges you to make **nutritious** desserts that contain less fat and sugar. Nutritious foods give you **energy**. The recipes in this book are made mainly from fresh ingredients such as fruit, eggs, yogurt, and milk. You'll be eating delicious desserts that your body can use to make long-lasting energy.

## You'll love our desserts!

The children you see in this book have tried our recipes and loved how they tasted! We know that you, too, will love them. These desserts taste so good that you won't miss the extra fat and sugar you might be getting in other treats.

### Healthy eating
- Drink plenty of water. If your sweet tooth is acting up, you may simply be thirsty. Two great drinks to quench your thirst—and sweet tooth—are flavored waters and tasty **licuados**, which are fruity shakes (see page 5).
- Choose desserts made with fresh fruit. Fruit contains natural sugar, so you won't have to add much extra sugar to your desserts to make them sweet.
- Watch your portions! You need only a small amount of dessert to satisfy your sweet tooth. Eat slowly and savor every bite.

# DRINK YOUR WAY TO HEALTH

One way to stay healthy is to drink at least six glasses of water a day. Water is the most important **nutrient** because more than two-thirds of your body is made of it. When your body is **dehydrated**, or needs fluids, you feel tired, hungry, and your muscles ache. You don't have the energy you need to think or stay active. Drinking water gives you energy. If you want your water to have some flavor, just add a few orange, lemon, lime, cucumber, or strawberry pieces. You won't believe how refreshing it will taste! Drinking naturally flavored water is an easy way to give your body what it needs and keep your taste buds happy at the same time! Make sure you wash the fruit first!

*Add a few slices of strawberry, cucumber, or orange with the peel on, to a bottle or glass of water. Allow the water to stand for ten minutes and drink up!*

## Smooth drinks!

Licuados are fruity shakes from Central America that are good for your bones and are better than sports drinks for adding fluids to your body. These shakes taste so good that you will want to drink them instead of eating dessert! The basic ingredients for 2-3 servings are:

- 1½ cups (375 ml) low-fat milk or soy beverage
- 1 cup (250 ml) ice
- 1 cup (250 ml) fruit (berries or pieces of melon, peach, pineapple, kiwi, or pear)
- 1 banana (can be used with other fruit or alone)

Put all the ingredients into a blender and blend. Licuados are great for breakfast and snacks as well.

# CAUTIOUS IN THE KITCHEN

Cooking is fun, but it can also be dangerous if you are not careful. When you are using an oven, stove, knife, blender, or food processor, make sure there is an adult in the kitchen with you. Accidents such as burns and cuts can happen quickly! **Allergies** are another common food-related problem. Before you start cooking, have an adult who knows your allergies check over each recipe's ingredients. Some foods may contain hidden ingredients such as nut oils. If you are allergic to nuts, be careful to read the labels on foods such as dried fruits and seeds. Nut oils can be found in many **processed foods**.

*Make sure you know how to use a blender, knife, oven, or food processor before you begin.*

## More safety tips

• Before and after handling food, use detergent and water to wash all your working surfaces, such as cutting boards and countertops. Then wash your hands.

• Always wash your hands with soap and warm water after handling eggs. When washing up, include your palms, the backs of your hands, your fingertips and nails, and between your fingers. How long do you wash your hands? As you soap your hands, sing the Happy Birthday song to the end. Then rinse your hands with warm water.

• Be sure to wash any raw fruits or vegetables thoroughly before you cook or eat them. Wash fruits that you peel as well, such as oranges, bananas, and pineapples. Also wash lemons and limes before you cut and squeeze them.

• Always wear oven mitts when putting food into or taking food out of the oven.

• Turn the handles of pots away from the edge of the stove so you don't knock them accidentally and spill hot food on yourself or others.

• Always use caution while preparing or cooking food.

# COOKING TERMS

When preparing the recipes in this book, you may see some cooking **terms**, or words, that aren't familiar to you. The pictures shown here illustrate some of these terms. The recipes include metric measurements in brackets. The letter "l" stands for **liter**, and the letters "ml" mean **milliliter**. When you see the words **teaspoon** or **tablespoon** without metric amounts beside them, you can use an ordinary teaspoon or tablespoon from your kitchen. In fact, many of the ingredients in this book don't have to be measured exactly. We use terms such as **sprinkle**, **dash**, **drizzle**, **pinch**, and **handful**. When you see these words, you can use an amount that is more or less than the amount stated in the recipe.

*purée/blend*: blend food into a smooth paste

*simmer*: cook gently so food bubbles but does not boil

*whisk together*: blend well using a whisk or fork

*handful*: an amount that fits in your hand

*sprinkle*: scatter solid or liquid particles over food

*core*: remove the seeds and stem from fruit

*slice, chop, dice*: cut food into even pieces

*whip*: blend with a mixer until peaks form

*toothpick test*: check if food is cooked in the center

*drizzle*: allow liquid to flow in a thin stream

# FUN WITH FRUIT

Use your imagination to create some great desserts and invite your friends to sample your creations. Fruit is naturally sweet and is loaded with **vitamins**, **minerals**, and **enzymes**. Try some of these fun ways to enjoy fruit or invent your own fruity desserts.

## Fruit Salad

Wash, peel, and cut some of your favorite fruits into bite-sized pieces. Make a salad of fresh fruits and add a few pieces of dried fruits such as dates, raisins, or dried cranberries. Wash the dried fruits, too! Dried fruits are very sweet and contain important minerals. For extra flavor, squeeze a little lemon or lime juice on your salad.

## A "peary" delicious treat

What can you do with a pear? Dress it up and sing it a song—what was that song about a "partridge in a pear treat?" To make this simply super dessert, cut a pear in half and take out the seeds. Put a spoonful of plain yogurt down the middle of each half and place slices of some other fruit, such as grapes or strawberries, over the yogurt. Drizzle on a little chocolate sauce, and you have a dessert to sing about!

# Fruit Kebabs

To make fruit kebabs, cut up your favorite fruit and thread it onto wooden skewers to make a colorful arrangement of fruit that is as artistic as it is delicious. Make a dipping sauce using pineapples and raspberries.

1 To make the pineapple sauce, place about one cup (250 ml) of pineapple chunks in a blender and purée.

2 To make the raspberry sauce, mash about a cupful of fresh or frozen raspberries with a fork.

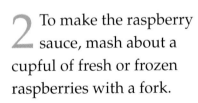

3 Using the mashed raspberries, put a "smile" into the pineapple sauce. Dip your fruit kebabs into this beautiful blend of sweet sauces.

# BAKED APPLES

Apples smell so good while they are baking that you'll have trouble waiting for them to be done! As an added bonus, your house will smell wonderful for hours. Keep your windows closed, or you might have some unexpected guests drop in to share your dessert!

**For four people, you need:**
- ½ cup (125 ml) raisins or dried cranberries
- 3 tablespoons (45 ml) chopped walnuts or almonds
- 1 teaspoon (5 ml) grated lemon **rind**, or peel
- 1 teaspoon (5 ml) cinnamon
- 4 teaspoons (60 ml) brown sugar or pure maple syrup
- 4 apples
- water

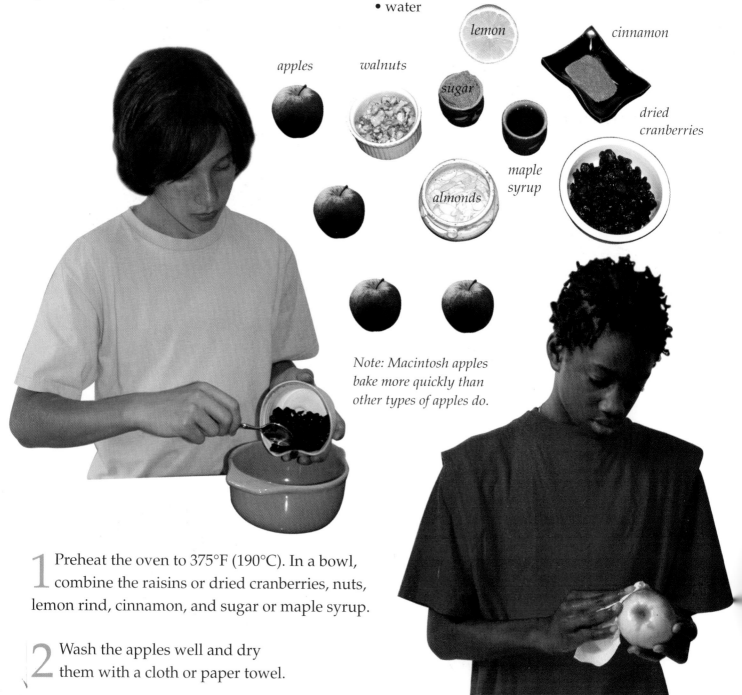

apples

walnuts

lemon

sugar

cinnamon

almonds

maple syrup

dried cranberries

*Note: Macintosh apples bake more quickly than other types of apples do.*

1 Preheat the oven to 375°F (190°C). In a bowl, combine the raisins or dried cranberries, nuts, lemon rind, cinnamon, and sugar or maple syrup.

2 Wash the apples well and dry them with a cloth or paper towel.

3 Core the apples but do not cut through the bottoms. Get an adult to widen the opening of each apple with a knife so there is plenty of room for the filling.

4 Ask an adult to score the apples about halfway down, as shown below. Scoring the apples will allow them to expand as they bake.

5 Place the apples in a baking dish. Spoon an equal amount of filling into each apple. Add enough water to cover the bottom of the pan.

6 Bake for 30-40 minutes or until the apples are soft and mushy. Baking time for soft apples is 20-30 minutes.

7 Cut each apple in half and serve the dessert warm with an extra sprinkle of cinnamon.

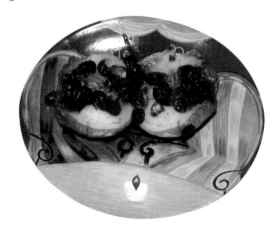

# FRUiTY iCE PoPS

If someone gave you a glass of juice and said it was dessert, you'd probably feel cheated, but freeze the same juices and you will have a delicious—and healthy—dessert! For a refreshing tropical treat, start with a banana, add some pineapple juice, and top it off with coconut milk. If you like the taste of chocolate, add a teaspoon of cocoa powder to the juices. To make a really simple frozen ice pop, just pour your favorite juice—mango, peach, pineapple, or berry—into molds. Unsweetened juices are healthier choices than sweetened juices.

**To make 4 tropical ice pops, you need:**
- 1 banana
- 1 cup (250 ml) pineapple juice
- 1 cup (250 ml) coconut milk
- 1 teaspoon (5 ml) unsweetened cocoa powder (optional)

1 Put the banana into a blender. Add the pineapple juice and coconut milk. Blend well.

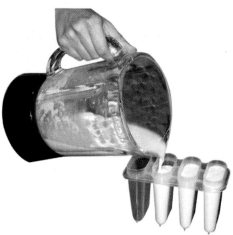

2 Pour the mixture into ice-pop molds, filling them almost to the top.

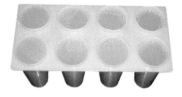

*Make juice pops using one or more kinds of juice such as orange, berry, or mango.*

3 Cover the molds with their tops, which contain the sticks. The juice will freeze around the sticks. Let the ice pops freeze overnight.

4 When the juice is completely frozen, run the molds under warm water until the ice pops can be pulled out easily.

*(left to right) Valeria decided to make a banana-coconut-pineapple-chocolate ice pop, Jennifer made a mango-juice ice pop, and Erika made an ice pop using berry juices. Which flavor will you make? The choices are endless, and the delicious tastes will surprise you! Make some for your parents and friends, too. Maybe your sisters will let you sample theirs.*

# CHOCOLATE MACAROONS

These cookies are extra easy to make because you don't even have to bake them! They taste great and contain nutritious ingredients—oats, coconut, milk, and walnuts! You'll love these cookies anytime or anywhere! To share with a friend, always carry a spare.

**To make 12 macaroons, you need:**

- 1½ cups (375 ml) quick-cooking oats
- ½ cup (125 ml) unsweetened shredded coconut
- ¼ cup (62 ml) chopped walnuts
- ½ cup (125 ml) sugar
- ¼ cup (62 ml) milk
- ¼ cup (62 ml) butter
- 3 tablespoons (45 ml) unsweetened cocoa powder

1 In a medium-sized bowl, combine the oats, coconut, and walnuts. Set aside.

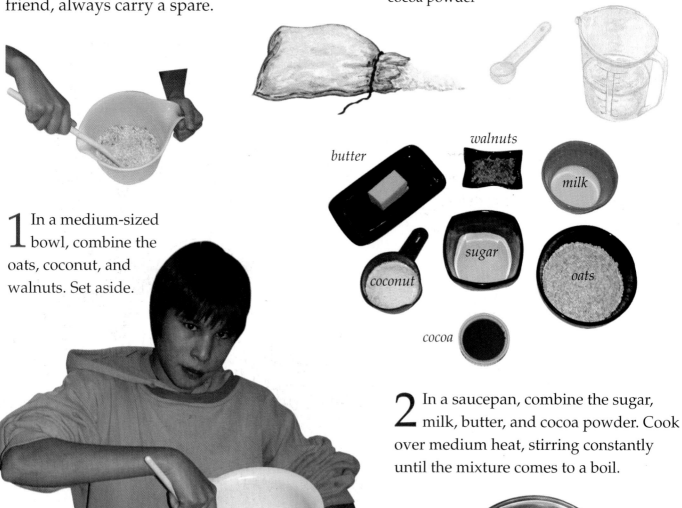

*butter*  *walnuts*  *milk*  *sugar*  *oats*  *coconut*  *cocoa*

2 In a saucepan, combine the sugar, milk, butter, and cocoa powder. Cook over medium heat, stirring constantly until the mixture comes to a boil.

**3** Remove the chocolate mixture from the stove. Be sure to wear oven mitts when you are carrying a hot pot!

**4** Stir the oat mixture into the pot containing the hot cocoa mixture.

**5** Quickly drop the mixture onto waxed or parchment paper, using two teaspoons to form the cookies.

**6** Cool the cookies completely in the refrigerator before serving them. You'll love these chocolate-y chewy treats!

# THE BEST ICE CREAM—EVER!

Did you know that a three-scoop ice-cream cone contains as much fat as five regular cheeseburgers? Banana ice cream tastes just as delicious as the ice cream you buy at the ice-cream parlor, but it has no added sugar and contains very little fat. It sounds too good to be true, but it is! You can eat it plain or flavor it with berries or cocoa powder. You can also make an ice-cream sundae by adding other fruit, a sprinkle of nuts, or a little chocolate sauce. Make your own creations!

**For two servings, you need:**
- 3 frozen bananas
- ¼ cup (62 ml) 5% or 10% cream

1 Peel and freeze some ripe bananas. Always keep some frozen bananas handy because they make excellent ice-cream treats or shakes.

2 Allow the frozen bananas to thaw about 5 minutes or until they are easy to cut. Cut them into bite-sized pieces, as shown above.

3 Put the bananas into a food processor with the cream and blend until the mixture looks like ice cream.

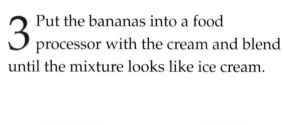

16

To make strawberry-banana ice cream, add a few strawberries to the banana ice cream. Don't stop there! You can make pineapple, raspberry, blueberry, cantaloupe, and peach ice cream, too. Just add about a half cup (125 ml) of fruit to the ice cream.

To make chocolate ice cream, add a teaspoon or two (5-10 ml) of cocoa powder. You won't believe the chocolate-y goodness!

*strawberry-banana ice cream*

To make an ice-cream sundae, put raspberry sauce on the ice cream. Just mash some fresh or frozen raspberries.

*chocolate-banana-strawberrry ice cream*

You can add nuts to your sundae as well. If the ice cream has melted, just put your sundae into the freezer for a half hour before eating it.

*chocolate-banana ice cream*

**Allergy alert! Before making the sundae on the right, be sure you are not allergic to walnuts.**

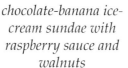

*banana sundae with raspberry sauce*

*chocolate-banana ice-cream sundae with raspberry sauce and walnuts*

# APPLE-RASPBERRY CLOUD

You'll be on cloud nine when you sample this dessert! It is light, sweet, creamy—and so easy to make. Do not use real egg whites because raw eggs can contain bacteria called **salmonella**, which can make you very sick. You can find **pasteurized** egg whites in cartons in the **dairy** section of your supermarket—right near the whole eggs. They are safe to eat.

**To make 4-5 desserts, you need:**
- 4 medium-sized apples
- ½ cup (125 ml) apple juice
- 1 teaspoon (5 ml) lemon juice
- 1 cup (250 ml) raspberries
- ⅓ cup (85 ml) pasteurized egg whites

1 Wash the apples well. Peel, core, and chop them into pieces.

2 Put the apples into a cooking pot with the apple juice and lemon juice. Simmer until they are soft and mushy.

4 Mash the raspberries using a fork and add them to the applesauce.

*Peeling apples is quick, easy, and fun when you use an apple peeler—and you can make glasses using the peel!*

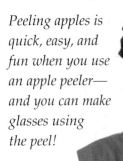

3 Allow the cooked apples to cool and then put them into a food processor. Purée the apples to make applesauce. If you have no time to make applesauce from scratch, use 2 cups (500 ml) of bottled unsweetened applesauce.

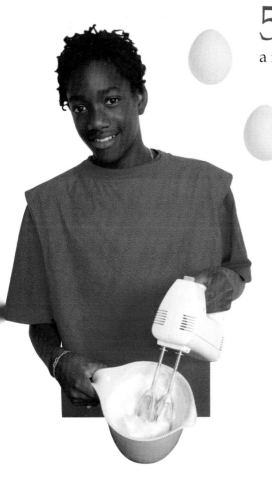

5 Place the egg whites in a bowl and whip them with a mixer until white peaks form.

6 Gently fold the whipped egg whites into the apple-raspberry purée.

*Note: Eat this dessert on the day that you make it and discard any leftovers.*

7 Serve the apple-raspberry cloud in individual dessert glasses. Refrigerate for 30 minutes before serving. You'll love this dreamy dessert!

# FRUiT CUSTARD

**Custards** are puddings made with milk and eggs. Our custard is made with fruit as well. It is very low in fat and sugar and will give you lasting energy. Enjoy it hot or cold. You can even have it for breakfast! It is a great dessert to make during cherry season. If you cannot find cherries at the fruit market, use apples and cranberries instead. Your custard will taste just as wonderful!

**To make 6-8 servings, you need:**
- 2 cups (250 ml) cherries or sliced apples (use a handful of cranberries with the apples)
- 3 tablespoons (45 ml) sugar (see step 4)
- 4 eggs
- 2 cups (250 ml) low-fat milk
- 3 tablespoons (45 ml) flour
- 1 teaspoon (5 ml) vanilla
- 1 teaspoon (5 ml) nutmeg

**1** Preheat the oven to 350°F (175°C).

**2** While the oven is heating, wash the cherries and pat them dry with a paper towel. Then take out their pits.

**3** Arrange the cherries evenly on the bottom of an ovenproof dish.

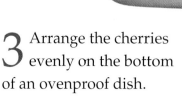

*If you are using apples instead of cherries, peel, core, and cut them into thin slices. Put the apple slices into an ovenproof dish. Dot the apples with cranberries, as shown right.*

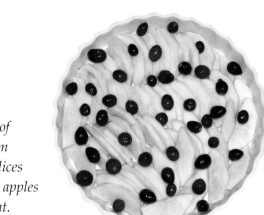

**4** Sprinkle the sugar evenly over the fruit. Use **raw** sugar if you can. Raw sugar has large granules and is gold in color because it has not been **refined**.

**5** Pour the eggs, milk, flour, vanilla, and nutmeg into a blender and blend until the mixture is creamy.

**6** Pour the mixture over the fruit and place the custard in the oven. Make sure you are wearing oven mitts!

**7** Bake the custard for 40-50 minutes. Do a toothpick test to see if it is cooked all the way through.

**8** Allow the custard to sit for 5 minutes. Scoop out a portion with a large spoon and enjoy. You will love the wonderful aroma and taste!

*Note: Refrigerate any leftovers.*

# CHOCOLATE-COVERED FRUIT

There is nothing more delicious than chocolate-covered fruit! When you prepare it, your kitchen will smell like a candy store. Chocolate-covered fruit can be very expensive to buy, but you can make it easily and cheaply. This version has an added benefit of containing very little fat or sugar. It contains no whipping cream or corn syrup, which are usually found in store-bought versions of this dessert. You can use almost any kind of fruit—we have chosen strawberries and sweet cherries. Chocolate-covered banana, pineapple, and orange or mandarin pieces also taste great.

**For four servings, you need:**
- 12-16 fresh strawberries
- 16-20 fresh, sweet cherries (or pieces of other favorite fruits)
- 6-8 semi-sweet baking-chocolate squares

1 Wash, dry, and prepare the fruit you are going to use. If you are using cherries, leave on their stems. If you are using strawberries, do not remove their leafy parts. To use bananas, peel them and cut them into large chunks.

2 Melt the chocolate over low heat on the stove in a heavy-bottomed saucepan or in a **double boiler**. A double boiler is made up of two pots—one sits inside the other. Pour enough water into the outer pot to cover the bottom. Heat the water until it begins to simmer, but do not let it boil. Place the inner pot, which contains the chocolate, into the outer pot. The chocolate will melt slowly without burning.

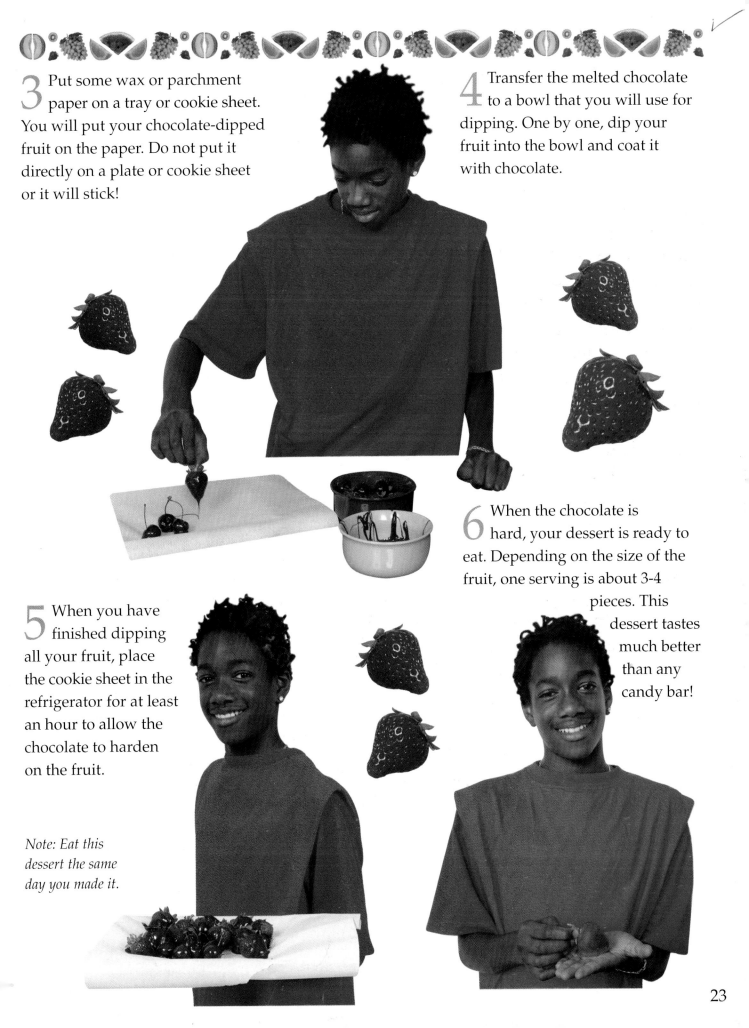

3 Put some wax or parchment paper on a tray or cookie sheet. You will put your chocolate-dipped fruit on the paper. Do not put it directly on a plate or cookie sheet or it will stick!

4 Transfer the melted chocolate to a bowl that you will use for dipping. One by one, dip your fruit into the bowl and coat it with chocolate.

6 When the chocolate is hard, your dessert is ready to eat. Depending on the size of the fruit, one serving is about 3-4 pieces. This dessert tastes much better than any candy bar!

5 When you have finished dipping all your fruit, place the cookie sheet in the refrigerator for at least an hour to allow the chocolate to harden on the fruit.

*Note: Eat this dessert the same day you made it.*

23

# JUMPING JELLIED FRUIT

The best thing about this dessert is that you can make it with your favorite fruit and juice. It contains no **artificial ingredients** or added sugar. Suggested juices are raspberry, apple, strawberry, cranberry, or white grape juice. These juices will allow you to see the fruit in the gelatin. This recipe is just as easy to make as the packaged version of this dessert, but it is so much more delicious! Enjoy it on a hot summer day or anytime.

**To make four servings, you need:**
- 1 cup (250 ml) fresh fruit (strawberries, grapes, oranges, kiwi) and a few dried-fruit pieces such as dates, prunes, or raisins
- 2 cups (500 ml) juice, any flavor
- 5 packets of unflavored gelatin
- ½ cup (125 ml) cold water

1 Slice the fruit and spread it on the bottom of a gelatin ring or divide it evenly among four dessert glasses.

2 Pour the juice into a saucepan and bring it to a boil over medium heat.

3 In a separate bowl, add the gelatin to the cold water and stir well.

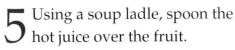

5 Using a soup ladle, spoon the hot juice over the fruit.

4 Lower the heat on the stove and slowly pour the diluted gelatin into the saucepan. Stir for about one minute.

6 Place the bowl or glasses into the refrigerator for several hours to allow the gelatin to set.

*Note: Eat this dessert within two days.*

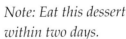

7 When the dessert wiggles but does not run if you tilt the glass, it is done. It's time for you to enjoy it yourself or share it with a sister or friend!

25

# HONEY AND NUT TREATS

When eaten together, honey, nuts, and yogurt are absolutely delicious and so good for you! They are especially healthful if you use the right type of ingredients. When choosing yogurt, buy a brand that contains **live bacterial culture**, which is something your body needs. Walnuts are great for your heart! Choose raw unsalted walnuts. If you eat this dessert a few times a week, you will do good things for your body and keep your taste buds humming!

*Caution! Before making the desserts on these pages, be sure you are not allergic to the nuts used in the recipes. Do not give honey to children under five years of age!*

**For a single serving, you need:**
- 1 cup (250 ml) plain yogurt
- 1-2 tablespoons (15-30 ml) walnuts
- 2 teaspoons (10 ml) honey

2 Sprinkle on the walnuts. Chop them first, if you wish.

1 Spoon the yogurt into a parfait glass.

**3** Drizzle on the honey. It's fun watching it flow onto the nuts.

**4** Enjoy this sweet treat and give thanks to the bees!

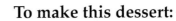

## Honey-Nut-Apple Snacks

This dessert or snack is very easy to make and tastes great! You can use any nut butter, such as peanut, almond, or hazelnut. Another way to enjoy nuts and honey is to drizzle some honey on the apple pieces first and then dip them into finely chopped walnuts. So yummy!

### To make this dessert:

1. Core and slice an apple into sections. An apple corer and slicer does a great job!
2. Spread a thin layer of nut butter on the apple pieces.
3. Drizzle a little honey on the nutty apples.
4. Enjoy this tasty—and healthy—snack.

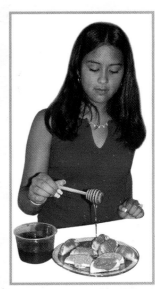

# SWEET-POTATO PIE

This wonderful pie tastes like pumpkin pie, but it has a much more delicate flavor. It is very easy to make. Sweet potatoes are naturally sweet, so each serving of the pie has less than two teaspoons of added sugar. We guarantee that it will be one of your favorite desserts!

**To make a pie (8 servings), you need:**

- one large or two small sweet potatoes
- one 9-inch (23 cm) deep-dish pie crust
- ¼ cup (62 ml) brown sugar
- ¾ cup (185 ml) low-fat milk
- ½ teaspoon (2.5 ml) nutmeg
- ½ teaspoon (2.5 ml) cinnamon
- ¼ teaspoon (1 ml) baking powder
- ¼ teaspoon (1 ml) salt
- 1 egg
- 1 tablespoon (15 ml) grapeseed, walnut, coconut, or other healthy cooking oil

1 Wash one large or two small sweet potatoes well and place them in a pot of water. Cook them on medium-high for about 25 minutes or until they are soft when pricked with a fork.

2 While the potatoes are cooking, bake the pie crust. Preheat the oven to 400°F (200°C). Prick the pie crust with a fork so that it does not bubble while baking. Bake the crust for 10-12 minutes. When it is golden brown, it is done. Allow it to cool.

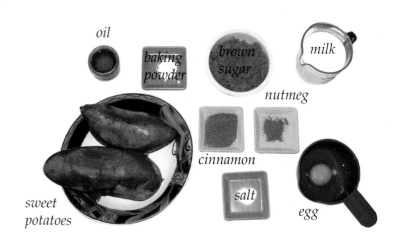

oil

baking powder

brown sugar

milk

nutmeg

cinnamon

salt

egg

sweet potatoes

4 When the potatoes have cooled, peel the skins off using your fingers, as shown below. Mash the potatoes with a potato masher and measure out one cup.

3 Lower the temperature of the oven to 350°F (175°C).

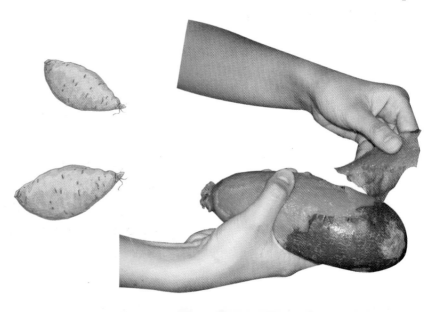

**5** Put the potatoes, brown sugar, and milk into a mixing bowl. Blend in the nutmeg, cinnamon, baking powder, and salt. Mix well.

**7** Pour the mixture into the baked pie crust and bake the pie for 50-60 minutes. Do a toothpick test to see if it is done.

**6** Using a fork or whisk, beat together the egg and oil. Add them to the other ingredients.

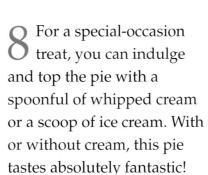

**8** For a special-occasion treat, you can indulge and top the pie with a spoonful of whipped cream or a scoop of ice cream. With or without cream, this pie tastes absolutely fantastic!

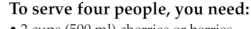

# BERRY BRÛLÉE

A **brûlée** is a dessert made using egg yolks. It has a hard top of **caramelized**, or melted and hardened sugar. Brûlées are normally difficult to make and contain a lot of sugar and fat, but our brûlée is just the opposite. It is is easy to make and is low in fat and sugar. Use strawberries, raspberries, cherries, or a combination of fruits.

**To serve four people, you need:**
- 2 cups (500 ml) cherries or berries such as raspberries, blueberries, or strawberries
- ⅔ cup (165 ml) sour cream
- ⅔ cup (165 ml) plain yogurt
- 1 teaspoon (5 ml) vanilla extract
- 4 tablespoons (60 ml) raw sugar

1 Preheat the oven's broiler to high.

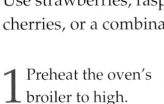

3 If you are using cherries, take out their pits.

4 If you are using strawberries, pull off their leafy parts and cut the berries into bite-sized pieces.

2 Wash the fruit well under running water. Then drain off the water.

5 Divide the fruit to make four equal servings. Place each serving into individual ovenproof dishes.

6 Mix together the sour cream, yogurt, and vanilla.

7 Spoon the mixture over the fruit to cover it completely.

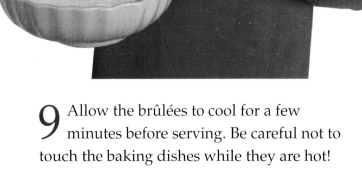

8 Top each serving with about a tablespoon of raw or brown sugar. Ask an adult to place the dishes under the broiler for 3-4 minutes or until the sugar has melted and turned golden brown.

9 Allow the brûlées to cool for a few minutes before serving. Be careful not to touch the baking dishes while they are hot!

# GLOSSARY

**Note:** Boldfaced words that have been defined in the book may not appear in the glossary. (Also see page 7 for cooking terms.)

**allergy** A sensitivity to certain foods that causes negative physical reactions such as rashes, hives, or difficulty breathing

**artificial ingredients** Foods no longer in their natural state

**caramelized** Sugar that has been heated so it melts and then hardens into a sheet of caramel

**dairy** Describing milk and foods made from milk, such as yogurt, cheese, and butter

**dehydrated** Describing a dangerous lack of fluids in the body caused by not drinking enough water or by losing too much fluid

**energy** The power your body needs to grow, move, and heal itself

**enzymes** Substances found in raw vegetables and fruits that help break down food, fight diseases, and speed up healing

**live bacterial culture** Growing bacteria that is helpful in breaking down food and removing waste material from the body

**minerals** Nutrients needed by the body; examples are calcium, which strengthens bones, and iron, which helps keep blood healthy

**nutrients** Substances such as proteins, vitamins, and enzymes, which are needed by the body for growth and repair

**nutritious** Describing food that gives the body energy and helps it grow and heal

**pasteurized** Food treated by heating for the purpose of killing harmful bacteria

**processed foods** Foods to which sugar, color, fat, or other chemicals have been added

**refined** Describing a food that has had its nutritious parts removed

**salmonella** Bacteria that causes food poisoning

**vitamins** Nutrients found in all fresh foods; vitamins A, B, C, D, E, and K are examples

# INDEX

1 2 3 4 5 6 7 8 9 0   Printed in the U.S.A.   3   2 1 0 9 8 7 6 5 4